# Intuitions

## Book of Poems

### Karl Kevin Smith

authorHOUSE®

*AuthorHouse™*
*1663 Liberty Drive*
*Bloomington, IN 47403*
*www.authorhouse.com*
*Phone: 1-800-839-8640*

*Published by AuthorHouse 12/22/2014*

*ISBN: 978-1-4969-5851-8 (sc)*
*ISBN: 978-1-4969-5852-5 (hc)*
*ISBN: 978-1-4969-5850-1 (e)*

*Library of Congress Control Number: 2014922244*

*Any people depicted in stock imagery provided by Thinkstock are models,*
*and such images are being used for illustrative purposes only.*
*Certain stock imagery © Thinkstock.*

*This book is printed on acid-free paper.*

*Because of the dynamic nature of the Internet, any web addresses or links contained in*
*this book may have changed since publication and may no longer be valid. The views*
*expressed in this work are solely those of the author and do not necessarily reflect the*
*views of the publisher, and the publisher hereby disclaims any responsibility for them.*

# Contents

# About the Author

My name is Karl Kevin Smith. I was born and raised in East St. Louis, Illinois. I am a proud by-product of the educational system of District 189. I was blessed to have some of the most brilliant teachers in my schooling years. English teachers such as Ms. Hunt and Ms. Dillard at Lansdowne Junior High School. Ms. Adams at Clark Junior High School. Mr. Logan at East St. Louis Senior High School. I just would like to thank these teachers for enhancing my life.

# Ode to the Mobility Air Forces

Only we can tell this story
Of our present and past glory
Made of walnut, silver and brass
With "fesswise" wings encased in glass

With strength of mind, body and heart
Never will our integrity depart
Our histories are rich in traditions
Of protecting the weak in precarious positions

Globally we go where few can dream
As our realities defy the imagination it seems
From land to air and all you can envision
That's when we begin to perform our mission

Impossible doesn't begin to define what we do
But we are honored to serve all walks of mankind too
We can never repay you for the sacrifices you gave
But remember the fallen as they slumber in their graves

We are all pieces to a puzzle with a role to play
Just as every minute on a clock completes a day
Many cannot comprehend the courage it takes to be you
Inconceivable to many but our job is never through

KKS

From:    Karl
To:      General Raymond E. Johns Jr
         USAF SAFB

# *Fallen Hero*

———◆———

There is no sacrifice greater
Than to give one's life in the theater
Memories where heroes now sleep
Not one tear will I weep

My comrade's mission is to take me home again
To be viewed by the masses, loved ones and friends
Tears welled in his eyes before he wept
But I accompanied him as I slept

As my hearse drove by I heard no cries
I saw no tears in mournful eyes
I was only content as it showed on my face
As I enjoyed my ride to my resting place

Never will I see battle again
Or bear arms with my friends
Or know the triumphs of victories of tomorrow
But not a tear will I weep for sorrow

Demise is now where I reside
With honor I accept this term with pride
Forever now will I enjoy my sleep
Not one tear will I never weep

KKS

From:   Karl
To:      General Raymond E. Johns Jr USAF

# *Mission Accomplished*

———◆———

Many seasons have come along
But you remained vigilant and strong
As you reflect upon the past
My have the years come fast

Through hard work and dedication
Conviction and preparation
You reached the highest level of success
That only few are invited to this apex

Your demands on yourself befriended new insights
Which exposed you to deeper farsights
That you shared with many as they now understood
Knowledge acquired is intellectually good

You have flown to many places
And seen so many faces
While always protecting your friends
From perils that knows no end

But the time has come to release the reins
To another and let him maintain
The path that you have traveled for years
With integrity and no fears

The brightness of your star will forever shine
As a rare diamond like you is a lifetime find
But your brilliance must be shared and shown
As you must leave us and move on

Mission accomplished sir
Mission accomplished

From:   Karl
To:      My friend Ray
           Sir have a great
           retirement
           21 Nov 12
           6:00 PM

           Karl Kevin Smith

# Soul

To look within
   The depths of self

And find a place
   Where the soul resides

Whether it be tall
   Or that of an elf

Does not diminish
   The contents of what's inside

                        KKS

# Butterflies and Angels

As lost love turns into unawareness
Butterflies and Angels feel the unfairness
Often the first victims to feel lost
A heavy price to pay for such a cost

Love runs away and leaves no address
While Butterflies and Angels endure more stress
Daydreams of thoughts of not being together
More hard times and stormy weathers

Butterflies and Angels cry into watery hands
For the definition of why that avoids understand
Float, float, float away pain and grief
As time will heal and give relief

KKS

# Beautiful Flower

Beautiful flower why do you cry
For future pains that confuses why
Beautiful flower why do you cry
For past beatings that blacken your eyes

Beautiful flower how did you break your arm
You blame amnesia for the harm
You shake your head as you disconnect
To erase the pain as you don't object

Beautiful flower you often reflect
Of years lost to suffering and neglect
Beautiful flower don't lose your aroma
Because your petals will fall into a coma

KKS

# *Thornrose*

Thornrose with your protective gears
Is it there to shield your fears
From harm done of yesteryears
Of jagged edges that forever sears

I'm not here to hurt your feelings
Or introduce pain that's not appealing
I talk to you without touch
For the pain you suffer must be much

I look at you and see drowning eyes
In cupped hands and muffled cries
I hope in time you discard your thorns
And be receptive to my charms

For I would never break your heart
As the butterfly knows mistrust must depart

KKS

# *Wilted Flower*

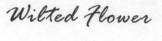

Once full of vigor and love
Your loyalty for your man stood above

With beautifulness adored by many
Lonely nights tears flowed aplenty

Loneliness do to neglect is a terrible plight
There are no excuses that could never make this right

Can a flower wilt from lack of saturation
Or die do to too much hydration

Wilt away flower as your life dies tonight
Photosynthesis never exposed you to any sunlight

KKS

# *Windows*

On the outside looking in
As necro begins to end a friend
This toxic concoction you call a cure
Russian Roulette they now must endure

Positive thinking my old new found friend
Mentally negotiating for time to extend
As their life begins to climax
Their journey with life begins to relax

For they have enjoyed seasons to remember
Many springs and many Decembers
They welcomes slumber with new dreams
Without remorses without screams

KKS

# *Waterfalls*

My eyes rain in my face with stormy tears
For the pain and love for you of many years

Today I see you in this state of mind
Tears cascade to express the pain that I find

For to see you in a shell of self
As I reminisce when you were someone else

I never forgot the joy you gave
Or the memories that I save

Your kindness was beyond reciprocation
As you put others first without manipulation

Your memories will always be treasured in my heart
For the love you gave will never depart

KKS

# *Lover's Addict*

I wake up thinking about you through the night
Chasing you wanting you and seeing your sight
Inhaling you smoking you and shooting you in my veins
Without you I'm in perpetual pain

I would walk through a forest fire to be with you
And swim in oceans full of tsunami(s) too
I would die twice in one night
To make sure that you are alright

I'm hooked on a sensation called you
Without you my world is through

KKS

# Almost Gone

Heated spoons and liquid mixes
Put in needles for our fixes
Your proclivities never tease us
As your habitualness begins to please us

Our minds open as the pleasure comes
Leaving us in a state called comfortably numb
A plethora of tracks on our arms
With each step closer to permanent harm

We slip in and out of a sleep like death
On step closer to no more breath

                                        KKS

# *Stormy Weather*

As I listen to your voice roar
In a car with closed windows and doors

My ears are held hostage to your diatribe
Of unpleasantries that you now describe

In my silent calm is where I reflect
Before my hurricane matures to collect

Everything caught up in this storm
Will pay the Piper with great harm

Feelings once verbally abusive will cease to be
As my ruthlessness is exacted brutally

On a paper tiger with no claws
Dressed in a skirt with menopause

                              KKS

# *Befriended*

Alone as the corner and I befriends each other
We begin to divulge secrets as though we are brothers
About acquired pains that we have went through
And a few good times that we cherish and acknowledge too

The conversations last for many hours
Of intellect of beauty, pollinated and flowered
Of the winter's when such flowers wilt and die
Bringing about broken hearts and eyes that cry

I found myself caught up in a cerebral daze
Recollecting memories unlocked from save
Corner puts its hand on my shoulder and articulates
As in life we all participates

KKS

# Humble Servant

Can a king be a servant with grace
To those who have abused him because of his race
Propaganda has created this infamous date
As deceptive pastels color his portrait

Deprived of decades of freedom's kindness
Left to be broken in a cage until death reminds us
But strong enough to endure the hardships of pain
Overcoming hatred with compassion not disdain

Reconciliation begins in one's heart
As past pains are forgiven to depart
Isn't it ironic that a man of innocence was incarcerated
Because he refused to be emasculated

KKS

# *Whisper's*

A soft voice
   Calls in the night

Desire's whispers
   Want leave you alone

Curiosity
   Refuses to sleep

Saying come closer
   So you can hear more

Before the
   Ambiance is no more

KKS

# *Peace of Mind*

Death by any other name
  Would be called
    Peace of mind.....

If I didn't have to
  Live with you anymore.....

KKS

# *Mix*

———◆———

Drowning yourself
    Inside a bottle to
        See if you can swim....

Where pain and
    Sorrow floats about
        Bubbling near the rim......

Now your version
    Of the truth stutters
        With a drunken tongue.......

Lie free thoughts
    Are a plenty as your
        Inhibitions have sung........

KKS

# Clash

Can the sheep avoid the wolf's arms
In this moment of mortal harm

Can the sheep negotiate with the wolf's appetite
And convince it that eating sheep isn't alright

Does bipartisanship exist in the world of these two
That makes compromise a reality to do

Or does the hunger of the wolf overrides
The intellect that the sheep now provides

KKS

# *Fell*

---

Even though I fell for you
With open hearts we connected too

Without past to erode our crescent
Trust and respect forever present

For I would move a mountain for you
So that you could see destiny's point of view

It's all about the happiness of you and I
Forever and a day until we discover demise

KKS

# *Headgames*

You play these twisted games
Manipulation and deceit are their names

You may find yourself all alone
Calling for a voice on the phone

Vanish feelings do exist
No reply is the verbiage I enlist

Feelings for you are numb to the core
As disappearing thoughts are seen more

KKS

# Optimus Idealus

Often you confuse us
Then you want to use us
Have you seen this
Just what is genius

Would you recognize us if you screen us
Or would you deny us after you seen us
Could you acknowledge the simplicity of our insights
And realize our visions are obtuse and bright

Or would you ridicule that which you couldn't understand
And later try to steal our ideas with slight of hand
Is it possible to get credit in the living years
For our creative works that now appear

Or would we have to die
Before you prostitute us after your reply

KKS

# *Swine*

———※———

Mr. Pigg with your shield
I know this trickery isn't real
Raise our hands up while you take our loot
Threaten to kill us with the bullets you shoot

Shake us down with your blackmail
Muted voices never tell
Hustlers and players are victims of your grind
Snitchery and bitchery topics on your mind

Mr. Pigg goes to court and testifies
With framed pictures for those he despise
Clandestine thievery your favorite pay off
Street taxation with no day off

Mr. Pigg why do you wallow
For every penny and every dollar
When you are caught will you fall
On your sword and end it all

                                        KKS

# Why?

Why would I ever play with your mind
And try to treat you so unkind
Why would I ever cheat on you
Abuse you and beat on you

Why would I tell you untrues
Just to make you sing the blues
Why is it you that I think about
Every second with all my thoughts

Why would I not want to be your man
I'll always listen and try to understand
Why would I not want you in my life
Today, tomorrow I'll always call you wife

KKS

# Talons

When the birds of prey
   Begin to slay
      The animals in the field....

We look about
   In confused thoughts
      As the carnage seems surreal....

Screams of agony
   Are muted only
      By death's soft hands....

We now observe
   As spectators as nature
      Picks the chosen from the land....

                                    KKS

# Glass of H$_2$O

Seeing you so full of sweat
As you perspire to keep wet

I look at your body and enjoy
The koolness that you deploy

Tasting you as I kiss your lips
With numbing touch after a sip

Rivers flow on tongue and cheek
As currents quench the thirst I seek

KKS

# 9mm

Many days and years I found pain and fear
As a broken soul drowned in a tidal wave of tears
Our children witnessed this with fearful eyes
Now older eyes have grown to despise

Brutality always kicked in my doors
Bringing horror and much more
Broken bones and beating almost to the last breath
Life no more please can I befriend death

Insinuations were the invitations to wreak havoc on me
Broken spirits and bones are the aftermath you see
So I swallowed a bullet to escape this plight
Now peace of mind at last maybe I can sleep tonight

KKS

# Sleeping Baby

Trapped inside a womb
Called tomb
D.O.A.
Before I could live a day
No pains no screams
Or even dreams
Did I fall asleep and wake up dead
Life no more visits my head
Outside the womb there is no life
I'll never be called husband or wife
Daughter or son
Or even know fun
I don't even know my name
Stillborn I am has taken its claim

KKS

# When a King Dreams

———❦———

Purple mountain's majesty
Non violence treated brutally
People of color found no humanity
As segregation was on the menu to be

The american nightmare continued to be
Deprivation of civil liberties
People of color found it hard to see
The definition of equality

Mistreated because of our skins
Will this nightmare always be our friend
With open eyes you try to comprehend
This never existed as you now pretends

A King dreamed this wasn't kind
Fairness should always be color blind
Racism is always unkind
Showcased only by mankind

When a King dreams of equality
That all people has a right to be
Devoid of hypocrisy and treachery
Then life would truly be equally

KKS

# *Perceptions*

Sometimes amnesia corrupts the truth
When we begin to describe the inner city youths
Most colored malefactors and perpetrators
No good found in them lost participators
It is indeed a grave misdeed
To color one as you perceive
But in this world of hard knocks
Where pain is found and crack rocks
There shines a beacon of light
Where intellect is employed day and night
On college degrees and PHD(S)
Which are manufactured within these miseries

KKS

# Lost Time

Time crawls on her knees
As she tries to avoid realities
Incarcerated for twenty five years
Eyes dried out from crying tears

Inside of a cage like a trapped bird
Freedom's thoughts are rarely heard
Hair once black turns all white
Some credit wisdom I credit insight

My clock stopped in 1999
After that my freedom resides in rewind
Twenty twenty four my new release date
Too many years finds so much hate

If there was ever a moment I could change
As 20/20 hindsight looks so strange
To act once and think twice
No crime committed wouldn't that be nice

                              KKS

# Change

You are as timeless as the universe
Whose beauty has become your curse
Jealousy often walks by
As envy's voice always sigh
Tears of remorse rolls down her face
While her hypocrisy wants to take your place
Confused and deluded as she must be
Only being you would cure her insanity

KKS

# *Sexy Overdose*

You float through an ocean in my veins
Creating euphoria in my brain
It's only you that swims through my mind
Exposing beauty never seen by find
As I visualize the aesthetics of your face
That uncovers itself from a darken place
With a physicality that only knows beauty
And a silhouette with a valentine day box booty
I'm a junkie overdosing in my mind
As this feeling I introduce to find
Before I die and open my eyes again
I will dream of you before my demise begin

KKS

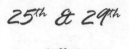

# 25th & 29th

I wish both my August born brothers happy birthday
I think of you everyday but especially on your death days
Songs that you like to hear
When on the radio catches my ear
I miss your fast minds and comedic ways
As we stayed up many hours laughing all day
I also miss the reality of your conversations
Straight to the point without hesitation
Every now and then I dream about you two
Dreams so real when I awake I start looking for you

KKS

# Dream (Dying in my Sleep)

Words cannot comprehend
A love that I cannot pretend
For a beautifulness that I only see
When I close my eyes tightly

My imagination cannot define
The textures that I find
When I touch the softness of your skin
As I reminisce again and again

Time stands still and freezes years
As your aesthetics are crystal clear
In a state where beauty is not confined
Timeless elegance well refined

Never again do I want to awake
Because I know that would be a mistake
Never again will I open my eyes
To be introduced to a painful good-bye

KKS

# Blown Away

Clouds, clouds you swirl about
Bringing terror and painful thoughts
Your coolness and hotness begins to form
Incubating a perfect storm

Winds blow and begins to twist
Creating dangers that now persist
Twisters you come and causes destruction
A by-product of your production

Many tears are spent but some we save
Windows pain and houses dwell in graves
Some of us hide from this devastation
As nature conducts another predation

Love one's lives are lost in this melee
As yesterday's sorrow turns into another day

KKS

# *Beautiful Demise*

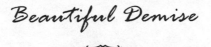

Today a flower wilts as sorrow tilts her head low
Pain begins to come and it doesn't want to go
Tears begin to flow as memories seem forever
Of such a beautiful flower whose presence will be never
Gone for a walk that only one can take
On a path called my time that no one else can make

KKS

# Physique

As you walk by with your aesthetic physique
Time stops and watches your beauty mystique
Art never posed in such a frame
Impeccable should be your name
Perfection viewed for all to see
As observers are intoxicated totally
Never have curves twisted with perception
As eyes moved about in all directions
Your beauty should be paraded in coliseums
And later showcased in all museums

KKS

# *You & I*

---

Pain whispered into abuse's ear
Why do we cause so much fear
Without you I can't maintain
To bring about havoc and disdain
The simplicity of our displeasures are plain
For we have destroyed many lives
Many peoples and many wives
Without you abuse I couldn't exist
But as long as we are together I must persist

KKS

# Antiquated

As time refuses to rewind
But many wishes it could find
A place in history
When many were treated discriminately

Our skin colors were a fatal attraction
As prejudice was the current fashion
Sick minds often manifested
Into cruelties that are detested

The downtrodden need not apply
Your helplessness will get a reply
You will be segregated because you are poor
As your dreams diminish when opportunity closes her doors

You sexual preferences are not my lovers
More hatred found as you will discover
Antibodies cannot override
Your disease that grows inside

Your ignorance only metastasizes
Against those that realizes
Your cowardice is inbred
And resides only in your head

KKS

# *Fall In*

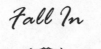

As You begin to paint another masterpiece
The leaves coordinate before they release
Into a spectacular vision to see
The beauty that autumn will come to be

God only You could have created this day
To showcase the artistry of leaves as they lay
Fall we realize your fashions are here
As you begin to change the year

Your pastels adorn the trees
While your winds blow a cooler breeze
Multi-colors that carpet the grounds
Million of designs awaiting to be found

Some put on flannels and other's sweaters
The essence of you can only get better
Pumpkins, strawmen and mums are in display
As halloween eventually will have its say

Leaves you run faster than some with two feet
To flee from the fire before you meet
Fall, fall you passionate friend
The essence of you should never end

KKS

# Lost & Found

You leave your family and wives
And now they must survive
The hardships of a concept
That leaves many looking for help

Fatherless as the story goes
Little hopes and plenty woes
Then realities begin to sink in
Wallow in pity or start new beginnings

These new thoughts run in their mind
Maturates and discovers find
Which unlocks the door of confidence
Where moving on has developed ever since

KKS

# Kindness 2 TK

You open your heart like no other
Kindness always shown to your brothers
Politeness doesn't begin to define you
As your kindness always shine through
As I fit in like a family member
Good times are all I remember
A trove of delectables
On the table of selectables
We feast and enjoy the eatings
Fellowship found by all at this meeting

KKS

# Sleep

Sleep that eternal sleep
Eyes closed no dreams to keep

No feelings as we feel no more
No life to keep no life to store

Sleep that eternal sleep
Loved ones cry and many weep

Still as we lay
As we have been promised this day

Sleep that eternal sleep
Into a realm beyond deep

Memories are cherished, present and past
No more life but peace at last

Sleep that eternal sleep

KKS

# SOS

Brutal beatings so unkind
Hides with demons of the mind

Seeks out help a long lost friend
Forever finding a long dead end

Painful thoughts are silence price
Hell served cold with lots of ice

KKS

# *Without*

---

If I can't have you then there will be no you
A twisted ultimatum only you construe
How can one neglect your point of view
A dangerous meal only served by you

On the menu of deceit and harm
Served hot, cold or even warm
Now you dine on your own recipe
Full of the venom that you had for me

Now you can walk away from me
With a new insight and humility

KKS

# Reverse (Antithesis)

When I adored you China Nice
You only treated me cold as ice

Now I treat you like a stone
Never will you leave me alone

Vanish feelings do exist
Ruthless charms she cannot resist

In her mind is where I reside
Invisible morals devoid her pride

KKS

# Lost

I forgot myself and my name
Without ID I must have came

Inside out I turn my brain
For clues of self that do not remain

I call for ego to help about
A shell of self in total doubt

For in myself a darken plight
Lost inside without a light

KKS

# 6

As I die within myself
In a body that is short of breath

I rest in a suspended state
As stiffness starts to overtake

I hear sounds so full of life
As death sings its final rites

I now begin my permanent rest
Sleeping inside a grave called self

KKS

# Broken

As we are dressed to kill
Our waiting time so tranquil

You promised again to share our day
As another excuse caused delay

The respect we had is no more
Of the dead promises that you store

Children always suffer the worse
Of an invisible father's syndrome curse

KKS

# *Diner*

Can one taste the beauty in love
While dining with a scintillating dove

A table set for two
In an area called rendezvous

We wear our thoughts in colorful guise
Intimate banter on the menu called surprise

We feast and dine on each other's anatomy
And finish the night with a dessert called flattery

                        KKS

# *You*

---

Wanting you with open heart
Times resting want depart

With you from black to grey
Enjoying your nectar everyday

Your curves they twist and never ends
From year to year always your friend

From eye to eye I falls right in
To see the depths of beauty again

KKS

# *Divers*

With eyes so deep can I swim
Was my reply to the gem

Her calm waters freed my tide
Cerebral raptures stirred inside

In and out pleasured thoughts
Enjoying feelings that we sought

KKS

# Betrayal

I trusted you with all
Even after you stumbled into a fall

Caught up in a web of double crosses
Selfish greed brought on your losses

Lies and deceit were just a few
Of the words used to blur your view

Instead of going in by yourself
You tried to take everyone else

Now its time to sit in that cage
Alone until the next Ice Age

KKS

# Selfish

Often you cause confusions
With your diatribe of conclusions

I look at you and often wonder
Do you ever try to ponder

About your rhetoric that is obtuse
Full of venom and verbal abuse

You are never wrong in your mind
Selfish one heart unkind

KKS

# Dish Cloth

You always use me at your leisure
Constantly treating me like a skeezer
Often I clean your plate
At home or when you're on a date

Dragging me through the debri and dirt
As though my feelings doesn't hurt
Should I be void of emotions
And never entertain commotions

You mangle and choke me but I never complain
I regroup, acclimate and still maintain
Never will I cry a tear
Because my place is always here

# *Contagious*

Every now and then I maturate
Into something that you hate
Many of my diseases have mysteries
That brings about catastrophe

I have lived centuries with demise
Your young and old will be compromised
I've developed immunities that destroy communities
And I don't need that many opportunities

Long time, short time you hear my alarms
As millions die from my harms
TB(S), HIV(S) and STD(S)
Are just a few of my good miseries

KKS

# River

That soupy gray river that drowns your dishes
My thoughts of thirst are no longer my wishes
Since you said retrieve a glass from that river
For self to drink in that makes me quiver

I observed a rat sip from that brew
And my answer to my thirst is still no thank you
How can one imagine touching such a waste
Full of residues and filthy paste

I know its time for me to go
But I'm afraid to put my feet on the floor

KKS

# *Excuse*

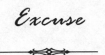

Is a reason you give yourself to do something....
Or not to do something....
Depending on the circumstances....
So that you can manipulate them to your advantage always....
That's all it is....

KKS

## C & H

Overflowing river brings about dryness
Eroding the landscape into wryness

New beginnings as the end has maturated
As life acclimates and often compensates

While we whince and hold our breaths
Spears prick a thousand deaths

Help floats in our veins
Caressing to alleviate pain

Sucrose has never been so sweet
But it brings a bitterness that makes some weep

                                    KKS

# *Thank You*

———◆———

You never suffer those who ask
On bended knees to know their task

We bow our heads with open minds
You deliver visions that we find

We praise and thank you for our blessings
While enjoying the beauty of Your lessons

KKS

# Serve

Yes I will serve the servant too
Because they are humans too

Place them on the same pedestal too
Because they have feelings too

Do not they emote as we do
Feel the pains and pleasures too

Yes I will serve the servant too
Because their time is overdue

KKS

# Confused

I thought I had arrived at last
But I'm going nowhere fast
And I'm in a hurry not to get there
The price of zero is the amount of the fare
As I ponder my next decision
My eyesight impairs my tunnel vision
As I ride inside my mind
Looking for self that's hard to find

KKS

# Grid

Off the grid is where I reside
No windows to view what's outside
Blank walls show the same scene
Monotony becomes so serene

Dreams run out of my head
Into a cemetary with the dead
Time moves at a slower pace
Twenty four hours become harder to face

Razor wires shave the sky
Clouds bleed as they float by
While I walk and labor on this concrete
My soul dies from the agony of defeat

KKS

# *Drifting*

A flower wilts and we know why
As nature comes and say good-bye
I float about in a room
Lifeless in a vase as you assume

As my spirit starts to leave
I see you cry and bereave
Your beauty is etched in my mind
Forever to envision easy to find

My love for you is all I conceived
As you reciprocated as I perceived
Drifting as I go away
All petals gone as I lay

KKS

# *Time*

---

Time the consummate thief
Takes no quarters gives all grief

Runs and runs and runs for fun
Never giving any refund

Patient enough to wait on you
To end all suffering just say you are through

Waits for all to close their eyes
To introduce them to demise

KKS

# Royalty

Mental games that brings on stress
As kings and queens clash in contest

Thoughts and ideas create new views
As diagonals and files open avenues

Bishops and knights die for the game
As pawns reincarnate into other names

As one king dies a lonely fate
The other rejoices in the splendors of great

KKS

# Character

Trust and respect was the cure
For the mortals to endure

Trust in dark oh so bright
Obstructs vision in daylight

Trust in self with strength of mind
Builds respect not hard to find

Always strong and never weak
Traits to honor that we seek

KKS

# *Open Doors*

As the doors begin to open
And the verbiage now is spoken

Of the past of things to be
History's true realities

Men's of past roamed to be
Kings of great societies

Full of genius that we see
As proof of structured technologies

The time has come to view your vast
And quench the wisdom of your past

KKS

# Hummingbird

The beauty of her words
Forever flows from the hummingbird

Neither pain or joy differentiates
The definitiveness that she articulates

For it's in her brain that ignites inspiration
Taking our minds into a voyage of fascination

Her words float, pierce and hit the mark
Rekindling emotions of dormant sparks

This lovely hummingbird never ages
As her wisdom lives forever in the pages

KKS

# Questions

How deep is the ocean
How wide is the sky
How deep is an emotion
That never questions why

What flavor is a kiss
When lovers taste and merge
Is ignorance truly bliss
When your IQ begins to submerge

Does an idea leave footprints
When it's running through your mind
Questions with many imprints
That's seen but hard to find

KKS

# Umbrella

Can I talk to you
And explain my point of view
Of what I think of you
Before the damage is through

When you walk in my shoes
I hope you don't find confuse
Sometime things get obtuse
When I visit with recluse

But I only love you
When everything is finally through
The reality of not being with you
Impairs my point of view

You are one of the chosen few
That I show my heart to
When tears drop like the rain
I think of you without pain

Sometime the clouds turn grey
And then they darken all day
So it's only true
You are the umbrella for my emotional rescue

# *Process*

---

Introspection knows reflection
Creative thoughts boundless directions

When I knock you know not when
Render paper employ pen

This door closing do come in
Bringing brilliance colorful friends

Subscribe now before I end
Capture visions that I send

KKS

# Memories

Memories of the morning dew
As blades of grass drinks from you
In this life of constant change
Many things seem so strange

Like what we did in younger eyes
Brought about constant surprises
As older eyes participate
Full of wisdom to acclimate

As new memories begin fresh starts
Older ones are cherished in our hearts

KKS

# Spectator

To live perhaps to taste
To watch perhaps to waste

To want perhaps to say
To do perhaps to delay

To seek perhaps to hide
And never enjoy the ride

For life has come and gone
Disappeared and left you alone

KKS

# A-Mer-I-Can

He graced spectators and gave them thrills
On the field he played with superior skills

Poetry in motion as shifted gears and sped
Leaving the game in his prime and moving ahead

His intellectual pursuits led him to Hollywood
Climbing that mountain top is where he stood

A man of compassion, wisdom and vision
Who objected against corrupted decisions

To pay homage and give this A-Mer-I-Can his crown
It's only fitting that we coronate you Jim Brown

KKS

# Snowflakes

Virgins fall from the sky
Without pain without cry

They accumulate in many places  .
At special times with smiling faces

Some think of them as being cold
While others enjoy as the beauty unfolds

As the land is covered with their whiteness
We are often blinded by their brightness

KKS

# *Fallen*

I fall from the heaven's above
Without halo without love

I kiss the sky from whence I fall
To reign supreme of gravities all

You know my name and why I speak
I will come and visit while you are weak

KKS

# *Retro*

Old and gray in my days
Doesn't excuse the past of yesterday
Can one go back and correct a wrong
For the pain and sorrow of years long

Brought about by a sickness called me
Exposed by a conscious of discovery
What I once had I never found again
Even through decades of illusions and many friends

How can one revisit the past of seems
While finding you at last in my dreams
Never does a day goes by
That I don't think of you and question why

Of the grief I put you through
And I can't go back to correct or undo

KKS

# Live

I die for self
And no one else
I will exhaust all breath
Before I entertain death

KKS

# Legal

Let me give you a lifetime of regrets
For investing in a lifestyle of smoking cigarettes
That tobacco leaf that you deem legal
Is the beginning to the end of an affair called regal

Let me thank you for the years of pain do to cancer
You are always in denial when questioned for an honest answer
Do tell the horrors of the coca and poppy plant
Illegal, banish not good for you say can't

I've never heard of second hand heroin smoke being harmful
to your health
But second hand smoke can accelerate your death
As my cigarette makes me sicker
Puff, puff, puff I die quicker

KKS

# US

Oh how I yearn for you
Burn for you
Turned on by you
Years have passed as I waited for you

To be with you
And only you
The time has come for this to be
For ourselves to see

Only you and me
The time right now is our present
Which is very relevant
To the completion of our development

There is no deception
Or rejection
As we understand with clear perception
Our love for each other isn't a misconception

                                        KKS

# *Recollections*

I've seen things that confuses seem
Sensations, emotions and many dreams
Lies, hypocrisies and ruthless ambitions
Famines, damnations and horrific conditions

Loves and dramas that human teaches
Billions and trillions that Wall St. reaches
Freedoms and dignities denied by design
Done by those arrogant and unkind

I've seen the life and death of John, Martin and Bobby
While their coffins were reposed in mournful lobbies
My isn't it ironic to revolve
From men to primates as we evolve

KKS

# Rather

I would rather wear a three piece pork skin suit
And walk into a den of hungry lions
Before I copulate over you and start lying
I would rather be a mangled jigsaw puzzle

Before I let you subdue my voice with a muzzle
I would rather stand alone and be a man
Than crawl on my knees with the masses
To accept an ultimatum and start kissing asses

That empowers you over me
Whether you be a man or woman
My principles are based upon my realities
And not your illusions of what my realities should be

KKS

# Home

Look at you dressed in red, white and blue
That brought about a revolution too
No taxation for the crown
We would rather die than bow down

You cradle us in your arms
Protecting us from all harms
At home and abroad
And you always make us proud

Often we think of you
Your glory and your beauty too
The quality of life that you give
In order for all to live

Your stars and stripes flow in the wind
As democracy's spirit will never end
Our eagle soars high in the air
While Lady Justice is blind but always fair

KKS

# Advantage - Love

How many dreams does it take
To eradicate the pains of racial hate
Physical that you see and feel
Economical that breaks your will

Dream on and cultivate your madness
Poison minds bring so much sadness
Young and old you're not exempt
From the ruthlessness of the racist contempt

Dream on until you awake
Not all are tainted and fake
But for those of you that harbor this sickness
I hope your antibodies kick in with the quickness

Ms. Racist why do you clutch your purse
Your misconception colors you worse
Cognitive of this fabrication all you life
While under the pretense of a righteous wife

When you wash yourself in lies
While wearing the mask of your guise
Only when there's an emergency cause
Do you put your racism on pause

Or when your life is on the line
Racism then lacks define
Now help is wanted by all
As the hypocrites anthem calls

KKS

# *Cold Front*

Freeze, freeze all your emotions
Without reasons or devotions

Commit yourself to no cause
Puppet of men of pause

You hides your head in the sand
Like an ostrich with no plan

Blinded by the snow in your nose
Icicles form as chill factor grows

KKS

# Slumber Not

From out of the heaven's the angel said
Ye of faith you are not dead
Slumber, slumber why do you sleep
God gave you His promise that He always keep
Mournful ones with teary eyes
I picked you to be with Me
To bring completion to your destiny
In My house is where you will be
With angels, honey and loved by Me

KKS

# Salutation Acknowledged

———⋈———

We are brothers and sisters in arms
Forever will we protect our country from all harms
Many of us are dedicated to this calling
As perils introduce some of us as fallen

Fear not as we will not surrender in the theatre
As we are united and no mission is greater
From ocean to ocean we will protect our waters
Forever and take no quarters

Our skies are protected by dynamic technologies
As our ground forces will introduce you to new realities
Everyday as we put on our uniforms
We cherish peace first before any harm

                                        KKS

# Eagle

A graceful ballerina with wings and flair
Floats about in the air
Soaring to heights of invisibility
That many of us will never see
Perfected to do this task
No excuses given no questions asked
Gliding about as though gravity doesn't exist
Soaring in the skies into heavenly bliss

KKS

# Cause and Effect

Missing you two
    with all my heart
But destiny has
    caused us to be apart
I see you every
    night in my dreams
But time has
    separated us it seems
I visualize the
    gift that beauty gave you
Aesthetics beyond
    the definition of adjectives too
My vision drove
    me to another path
Full of pain and
    relentless wrath
A global tour
    I traveled to live and tell
With many pitfalls
    leading to hell
But never did I
    give up on God and His plan
As I was blessed
    beyond the definition of understand
I miss you more
    than the procreation of my life
Beautiful daughter
    and lovely wife

KKS

# Window Pain

As I look
  at myself through a window pane
Where screams
  have an invitation with complain
Accompanied
  by whispers of no regrets
While confused
  ego stays upset
I'm trapped
  in a world of make believe
Where truth
  is used daily to deceive
Of things I
  thought were real I cannot conceive
As my perception
  has been detoured not to perceive

KKS

# Gladiator

Two men enter one man leaves
Life waits on death to conceive

On the battlefield were the gladiators fight
To the death even if it takes all night

Rips and tears as the body begins to die
No remorse for death no watery eyes

Pain never felt so good to feel
As death is delayed from the kill

The arena is filled with thunderous cheers
As death presence is acknowledge here

KKS

# Cerebral Emotions

I was
  accompanied by my best friend loneliness
He doesn't
  bother me as I begin to confess
About emotions
  that twist to and fro
Which are
  deeper than the ocean's floor
The scars
  in my mind float about and reminds
Of past
  memories that I rewind
Depths of
  pain I always find
Never discovering
  an emotion called kind
Cerebral nightmares
  only on the menu
Always on
  display as they continue
Holding my
  mind hostage in its cage
As I wallow
  in the bowels of its rage

KKS

# *Negotiator*

How can you
   negotiate with a toothache and cope
While praying
   for relief and trying to befriend hope
That it goes
   away forever and a day
Wishful thinking
   for one wouldn't you say
Until you free
   yourself from this pain
You can drive
   yourself totally insane
Medication can't
   be used for this plight
As pain invites
   more friends to your agony tonight
You ask God
   can you go to sleep and wake up dead
To bury this
   pain manifesting in your head

                                KKS

# 3:25 am

Chirp, chirp little birds
Your voices are always heard

In the morning when you bring
Beautiful melodies that you sing

As I listen to your voices
Multiple tunes of your choices

Every morning you are full of cheers
As your vocals are admired here

KKS

# Plain Jane

Plain Jane was her name she said
But her beauty was knock out dead
With a sexy body like an hour glass
And a personality full of class

In my imagination is where she use to be
Until she befriended invisibility
No reply is the language she used
As silence speaks loudest as deaf is confused

In time you might figure out
Loneliness is the choice you sought
I hope you find your tongue again
So you can rearticulate with your friends

KKS

# *Realities*

Let me take your mind hostage for awhile
As I introduce you to a unique style
Of realities that you hide in disguises
Which are full of untruthful surprises

Lies and deceptions reside within your reflections
As all is invited inside your perceptions
Truth never is invited within your mind
Clueless never discovered by find

You listen but you don't understand me
Because you can't comprehend my realities
Head doctors listen to my clues
Discovering deeper meanings within their trues

How can something as simple as being real
Unlock jealousies into a state of kill
I refuse to be untruthful and create alibis
And get caught up in a web of perpetual lies

KKS

# Intellectual Sociopath

I deprive my mind of all fears
As atypical thoughts are welcomed here
With a conscience groomed to find feelings
For oneself is so revealing

To visualize the imagination conjure such ideals
Leaves many in a state of perpetual surreal
But out of this comes intellectual thoughts
Creatively efficient beyond all doubts

You must think outside the box and push the envelope
That's the only way true genius is developed
In the solitary mind where ideals clash about
Do we truly understand the beauty of thoughts

Thoughts are never bad or good
Only what's extracted and understood
Just as death is only a comfortable sleep
And joy sometimes makes us weep

KKS

## OD

I love you like an addiction
Forever will you be my affliction
You visit me in my hallucinations
Daily without an invitation

Seeing you distorts my vision
Blurred reasoning confuses my decision
About what is real and what I feel
Of emotions that you never conceal

You reside constantly in my veins
Wreaking havoc but never will I complain
Broken hearted as I must be
But I turn the page and accept reality

Never again will you visit me
As I fell asleep permanently
In a place called good-bye
In a grave called you know why

KKS

# Fighter

Slowly death begins to weaken life
With body blows from constant strife
As life fights this losing war
It can see the impact of death's scars

Life's hair falls out of its head
As it scatters about in the bed
But never will life surrender to death
Until it has depleted all breath

To survive this life must master its fears
As death is always near
Waiting for you to give in
Wanting to become your new friend

But life fights to see another day
And continues to fight until it's okay
With strength of mind and will power
Life defeats death in the crucial hours

KKS

# Runaway

I decided to runaway and be on my own
Greyhound ran far and I thought I was grown
In this new city without any friends
Lint in my pockets and no ends

This episode went on for many days and nights
Until hunger kicked in and a few frights
I decided on my new occupation
Selling my body without hesitation

Many dangerous nights I walked the streets
Getting my grind on until my ends meet
I did things I never thought I would do
And gave up my money when I was through

Many years passed and my youth is gone
I dogged myself out a junkie all alone
I looked in the mirror for clues about what went wrong
So that I could call them up on the phone

To ask them how could I do this to me
And destroy my dreams and possibilities
I never knew one decision could destroy my world
As I recall memories now of being a little girl

KKS

# Skool

Crumbling buildings that we call schools
Wreaking with odors of a cesspool
We can barely get supplies to do our task
Which are invisible to us so why ask

This gantlet we go through everyday
Scars our mind as we struggles today
Many are gifted in areas where genius resides
But never given the address to find it inside

Negligence was the excuse given as the reason
As precocious minds rot on the vines every season
Repetitive boredom kills the spirit to learn
Just as leaves are harvested in the fall to burn

Your mind dies of mental atrophy
As lack of knowledge is designed to wither helplessly

KKS

# Fuse Box

In the spring this flower did bloom
But in the fall it met its doom
It was lost inside a body without a soul
No memories or feelings so very cold

Invisible friends I often talk to
Today, tomorrow or whenever we get through
Loved ones suffer when they see me this way
Every minute every hour as it turns into many days

I wish I could remember myself and then you
But vanished memories make this impossible to do
My fuse box is broken in my head
As it turns me into one of the living dead

KKS

# Wrapped Up

You got some pretty eyes
And within them there lies
A window where one can see
The definitiveness of your beauty

Your hands are softer than silk
And your finger nails are whiter than milk
Exposed is your silhouette
That is sleek and very select

And your figure is so curvaceous
Within a mind that's sagacious
And your total package is wrapped tight
Like a present on christmas night

With the ribbons and the bows
Forever does your beauty flows

KKS

# Be You

It's not my place to change you
Deconstruct you or rearrange you
It's not my place to reraise you
Hurt you or correct you

The only thing I ask is that you be you
Realistically and true
I'm not amused by sly lies
Or self induced crocodile cries

But I would appreciate your integrity
And willingness to endure its longevity
Even a chameleon doesn't turn into anything new
Maybe a different color or two

Only time changes in the spring and fall
And then it's still being real after all

KKS

# Fakery

Apparently you forgot the meaning of hypocrite
Full of lies as you marinate in complicit
As you have done the same thing
But pride helps you forget this one night fling

It's amazing how the accusations fly
When you think you have caught me in a lie
All I do is listen and pay attention
But I'll remind you what amnesia forgot to mention

That's about your present and what transpired in the past
As your memory begins to recollect at last
Don't take my silence for being unaware
As your devious mind operates with selfish care

When I start cutting into you with my surgical ruthlessness
Don't pretend to be confused, dumbfounded and clueless

KKS

# Ride or Die

Ride or die with you by my side
In you only will I confide
Through the peaks and valleys it is you I trust
As our loyalty will never tarnish or rust

My dreams and ambitions will be shared too
Today, tomorrow and only with you
No lies or alibis will never be entertained
Only the truth will be exposed and maintained

I'm with you from the beginning to the end
Until death do us part forever will we be friends
Ride or die with you forever and a day
Is my word to you until you decide to go your way

KKS

# John Boyd

How can we thank you for all you have done
As you treated us like your daughters and sons
Not once were we deprived of any
As you made sure there was aplenty

Your love was unconditional and never tough
But you thought that you wasn't doing enough
How generous can this person be
To introduce such logic verbally

Unconditional in his mind didn't know restraints
Or the definition of no or I can't
We love you more than the oxygen we breathe
Because without you we would wilt like leaves

We would take a bullet for you
Because your love has always been true
How could selfish ever understand
The definitiveness of such love within this man

                                        KKS

# Exhausted

Nobody sees me as a person
All my options worsen
Am I the ultimate cavity
No good drowning in depravity

How can I give you more
When I am a depleted whore
All money goes to you
No pride I am so empty too

I turned my back on me
Self induced miseries
Dilapidated, worthless where does my value begin
Living in a world of delusions that never ends

Many nights my soul was sold
In the dark where secrets were told
As I now walk the streets
Where only pain and sorrow meets

KKS

# Ice Trayed

I guess the world has become blind to see
Of the atrocity you committed visibly
As kidnapped from reality you must be
Your conscience wasn't employed that day I see

Racial profiling your point of view
Shoot to kill you want blame you
Hiding from the public your new technique
Eventually a muted tongue will have to speak

Racial mumblings under your breath
Was this the reason innocence found death
You changed a word into a new definition
To appeal to your ears and mental condition

Trayvon went to the store to by some snacks
But he wasn't able to make it back
Skittles and tea in his hand was his crime
As he walked out of life into no more time

KKS

Please accept my condolence for the loss of Trayvon. Who was
a rising star. Whose sparkle was taken away before its time.

Karl

111

# The Other Virginity

Death survives all it befriends
But we can live long but never comprehend
As life dies tomorrow and today
Death she greets us without delay

She outlives the definition we call infinity
As we are introduced to her virginity
She never tires as life permanently sleeps
Some disbelieve as mourner's always weep

But when we awaken from this cocoon
Will we be greeted by Jesus soon
Or will we forever sleep and dream
Never to find our way out of our grave it seems

If there is any doubt in our minds
Eventually we will all find
The answer to this question
Complete damnation or the beauty of resurrection

KKS